Psalmist Yvette Culver

For publishing information contact:

iamHisfoundation Publishing
P.O. Box 701072
Dallas, TX, 75370
888-958-2372
Yvette@iamhisfoundation.org

All rights reserved, including the right of reproduction in whole or in part in any form.

No part of this publication may be stored in any retrieval system or transmitted in any form or by electronic, mechanical, photocopying, recording or otherwise without the written permission of the publisher.

Cover Design
The Brass Effect: www.thebrasseffect.com

Editor's
Cynthia Henderson and Suzzen Stroman

Photography
Dorian Grant: www.dorianhgrant.com

Copyright © 2014 iamHisfoundation

All rights reserved.

Psalmist Yvette Culver

DEDICATED TO MY "SISTERS STANDING"

THE LADIES WHO HOLD ME UP WHEN I WANT TO FALL DOWN:

CAROLYN, CHAR, CHIFFON, CINDY, CYNTHIA, DARLENE, DINA, KEISHA, LAVON, PATRICE, SUZZEN AND SYLVIA

AND TO MY MORNING PRAYER CIRCLE:

BUTCH, LENITTA AND RALPH

LOVE YA'LL BUNCHES!

Introduction

Let me start by saying I never saw this book coming. Honestly… LOL. I was working on a different book, *Faith Walk*, when God dropped this little gem in my spirit. For the past two years God has had me on a journey of delivering poetry at conferences. Usually, I was asked to create a poetry piece specifically for a conference but on occasion, it was something I had already written and was then asked to share. In August 2014, I was driving home from work one day and I was talking to God about the direction of my life. Now, you may not get it, but I have "conversations" with God. Meaning I don't just go to God to pray to Him, I have a conversation with Him. God hit me with this: all of the poetry pieces I have written were *love letters* from God. Wow! Not only were they *love letters* from God, they were also a book of inspiration and devotion.

God also let me know that *love letters* was to be different than my first book *God Drops* or my work in progress book *Faith Walk*. You see, He was letting me off the hook for this book. I didn't have to reveal my life story. All I had to do was present what He had given me in poetry and monologues. And so that's what I did. So simple, yet so "God".

Psalmist Yvette Culver

We all have a story in us, but while this book is not necessarily my story, don't let that stop this from being yours. I have included blank pages at the end in case God gives you a *love letter* that you would like to write down. I am often approached by people who say "I have a great story to tell. I just need to write it. How do you suggest I start"? My reply, simply put…just start☺.

While editing this book I was also preparing to attend a 72 hour retreat. I had completed the changes and was going to send them to the publishing company and tell them the book was ready to print. But God instructed me to wait until after the retreat, so I did. The name of the retreat is The Great Banquet.

So I went to The Great Banquet not knowing what to expect because like one of my favorite movies, Fight Club, the first rule is, you don't talk about The Great Banquet. After completing the retreat, I now understand why. You have to experience it for yourself.

On my first night there, God gave me a new poem and told me that I would get a total of five before the retreat was over. And that's what happened.. After the fifth one, the well was dry.

The creation of this book has literally changed how I see myself. I have been waiting for God to reveal to me the calling He has for me. While reading a *love letter* at a revival this summer, God clearly spoke to me. I am His Psalmist. This was confirmed for me while at The Great Banquet. I am the quiet girl who would rather be in the background. But God has chosen me to write about His Glory. I've got to tell you, the moment God revealed that to me, it was another "of course" moment and it feels so right. The moment I received this confirmation, there was no turning back and I am not hiding anymore. I am all in.

So, God has changed my name…

Psalmist Yvette Culver

Table of Contents

1	Deuteronomy: *Blessing*..	8-9
2	Proverbs: *Curl Up*...	10-11
3	Luke: *Break Bread with Me*..	12-13
4	1 Peter: *The Fabric of a Godly Woman*...............................	14-15
5	John: *The Anchor*...	16-17
6	Matthew: *Did You Say Yes?*..	18-19
7	Daniel: *Being HAD*...	20-21
8	Hosea: *Gomer*...	22-23
9	Psalms: *Silence*...	24-25
10	Galatians: *The Fruit of God's Labor*.....................................	26-27
11	2 Samuel: *Hands Off!*..	28-29
12	Proverbs: *Breaking*..	30-31
13	Psalms: *Praise*...	32-33
14	Genesis: *Hagar*..	34-35
16	Deuteronomy: *Mirror Mirror*...	36-37
17	Esther: *Woman of God*..	38-39
18	Jeremiah: *Phenomenal*...	40-41
19	Romans: *Searching*..	42-43
20	Matthew: *Mary*..	44-45
21	Matthew: *Silent Saturday*..	46-47
22	Joshua: *Rahab*...	48-49
23	Ruth: *Ruth*...	50-51
24	Exodus: *Woman, Warrior, Worshipper*................................	52-53
25	Your Love Letters...	54-62
26	Blessings...	63
27	About the Author..	64

Psalmist Yvette Culver

My Inspiration

Sue Carolyn Hunter
1942-1990
Miss you mommie....

Jeremiah 30:2

² "This is what the LORD, the God of Israel, says: Write down for the record everything I have said to you, Jeremiah.

Note: *All Scriptures are New Living Translation Version*

Deuteronomy 28:1-3

*28 If you fully obey the L*ORD *your God and carefully follow all his commands I give you today, the L*ORD *your God will set you high above all the nations on earth. ² All these blessings will come on you and accompany you if you obey the L*ORD *your God: ³ You will be blessed in the city and blessed in the country.*

Blessing

Believe
Believe in He who you cannot touch, but can only feel,
He comes to you most when you lower yourself to kneel.
To have faith when you don't know the answers and are out of suggestions,
Move with His guidance without asking questions.

Love
Love truly and completely without reservation,
Ask nothing of those you love, without hesitation.
When I think of the love He gave to wash away our sins,
Loving others in His name, instantly makes me grin.

Exalt
Exalt His name because of his power until you can praise no more,
Remembering all the grace He brought you, once you opened the door.
To exalt is to praise, to sing, to dance and rejoice,
Who cares when you're done you no longer have a voice.

Serve
To be a servant is the ultimate acknowledgement,
This should be done without pain or begrudgement.
Serving is not always easy, it can involve some sacrifice,
But He served us His son, who else would pay that price?

Savior
We call Him Savior, Jesus, our rock, our protector in time of need,
In all honesty sometimes we just call on Him, Lord, come to me.
However, we must remember through trials and jubilation,
We must seek His presence through any situation.

Intimate
The love we have for God is an intimate relationship, it's different for us all,
It's the place we can laugh for no reason, cry for every reason and sometimes curl up in a ball.
When you're intimate with God, you can hear Him talk to you loud and clear,
Just close your eyes, clear your mind, and He's right there in your ear.

Need
God knew that we would need someone to stand in the gap for us, to show us the way,
To be an example for us to stand in the gap for others day after day.
When your need for God is strong and sturdy, it cannot be shaken,
He is our Father and we are His children, and our need will never be forsaken.

Go
I now challenge us all to go. Go and believe. Go and love. Go and exalt. Go and serve.
Go and call on our Savior. Go improve our intimacy with God. Go and profess our need for Him. Just go.
And the next time someone asks you, why do you praise him even when you are in pain?
Look them straight in the eyes and tell them,
Because praising God will break my chains.

Psalmist Yvette Culver

Proverbs 3:5-8

*⁵ Trust in the LORD with all your heart;
do not depend on your own understanding.
⁶ Seek his will in all you do,
and he will show you which path to take.
⁷ Don't be impressed with your own wisdom.
Instead, fear the LORD and turn away from evil.
⁸ Then you will have healing for your body
and strength for your bones.*

<u>*Curl Up*</u>

Feeling utterly alone and not knowing which way to turn,
I silently wished that the tears on my face wouldn't burn
Feeling helpless and scared to move, yet scared to stand still,
Not wanting to speak my thoughts, for fear they would be real.
You whispered sweetly in my ear, curl up on My lap My child.

Desperately searching for answers that always seem elusive,
Shouting out loud, tell me the plan, tell me the goal, I want to be inclusive.
One step forward, two steps back, two steps forward, three steps back. Why does it feel like my life is so off track?
You whispered sweetly in my ear, curl up on My lap My child.

Searching for a moment in time when things were at peace,
Crying out loud, what more do You want from me?
Obedience has been my pledge, even when it doesn't make sense,
Let me apologize, say You forgive me, let me get off the fence.
You whispered sweetly in my ear, curl up on My lap My child.

But my tears were blocking Your instructions, so You made it plain and clear, You, are my Father God.

But, You are my Father who takes care of me, You are my Father who nurtures me,
You are my God who created me, You are my God who sent Your son for me.

So I did as my Father instructed, laid my head on His lap and curled up, as I cried out to my God to put His arms around me and my Father, as I let Him comfort me.

My God is my Father, My Father is my God, but they serve a different purpose. So when you want that comfort, that safe place feeling,

Curl up on your Father's lap, as you cry out to your God.

Psalmist Yvette Culver

Luke 14:15-24

¹⁵ Hearing this, a man sitting at the table with Jesus exclaimed, "What a blessing it will be to attend a banquet[a] in the Kingdom of God!"

¹⁶ Jesus replied with this story: "A man prepared a great feast and sent out many invitations. ¹⁷ When the banquet was ready, he sent his servant to tell the guests, 'Come, the banquet is ready.' ¹⁸ But they all began making excuses. One said, 'I have just bought a field and must inspect it. Please excuse me.' ¹⁹ Another said, 'I have just bought five pairs of oxen, and I want to try them out. Please excuse me.' ²⁰ Another said, 'I now have a wife, so I can't come.'

²¹ "The servant returned and told his master what they had said. His master was furious and said, 'Go quickly into the streets and alleys of the town and invite the poor, the crippled, the blind, and the lame.' ²² After the servant had done this, he reported, 'There is still room for more.' ²³ So his master said, 'Go out into the country lanes and behind the hedges and urge anyone you find to come, so that the house will be full. ²⁴ For none of those I first invited will get even the smallest taste of my banquet.'"

Break Bread With Me

While you were sitting at your desk, I asked you to break bread with Me,
You said you were working on a report and only had 30 minutes left to finish so you didn't have time.
So I left.

While you were at your son's baseball game I asked you to break bread with Me,
You said there were three innings left and didn't have time.
So I left.

While you were driving to your doctor appointment I asked you to break bread with Me,
You said you were too busy thinking about your test results.
So I left.

So My beloved, I am done asking.

Had you taken the time to sup with Me the first time I asked, you would have had the report finished with ease.

Had you taken the time to sup with Me the second time I asked, you would have given Me thanks for the son you were watching play baseball.

Had you taken the time to sup with Me the third time I asked, you wouldn't have been worried about your test results for I am your God and had already given you a good report.

I have prepared a feast for you like none other.
When you are ready to sit at My table and enjoy the feast I have prepared just for you,
You will come to Me, and ask Me to break bread with you.

Psalmist Yvette Culver

1 Peter 3:1-6

*3 In the same way, you wives must accept the authority of your husbands. Then, even if some refuse to obey the Good News, your godly lives will speak to them without any words. They will be won over [2] by observing your pure and reverent lives.
[3] Don't be concerned about the outward beauty of fancy hairstyles, expensive jewelry, or beautiful clothes. [4] You should clothe yourselves instead with the beauty that comes from within, the unfading beauty of a gentle and quiet spirit, which is so precious to God.[5] This is how the holy women of old made themselves beautiful. They put their trust in God and accepted the authority of their husbands. [6] For instance, Sarah obeyed her husband, Abraham, and called him her master. You are her daughters when you do what is right without fear of what your husbands might do.*

The Fabric of a Godly Woman

It's the way I carry myself even when no one else is around,
When I think of His love for me I cannot feel down.
Each step taken with joy and pride with my head held high,
Everywhere I go, lifting my head to the sky.
It's my everyday walk that gives me the fabric of a Godly Woman.

It's how I treat others and show them true love,
Seeing someone down and simply giving a hug.
Offering to listen and really paying attention,
Sharing my story if need be, God's got me on a mission.
It's my everyday action that gives me the fabric of a Godly Woman.

It's praising Him loudly through the rising of the sun,
Studying the word that tells us how He gave us His son.
Knowing what I say can be powerful and cause infection,
Not allowing my words to be the sword of destruction.

It's my words that give me the fabric of a Godly Woman.

It's how I love to be in His presence and go before Him often,
Knowing that through God any hardship can be softened.
Staying strong in my faith and putting Him first,
Knowing that His love for me fills my thirst.
It's my love for God that gives me the fabric of a Godly Woman.

The Fabric of a Godly Woman, is me.

Psalmist Yvette Culver

John 14: 15-21

¹⁵ "If you love me, obey[d] my commandments. ¹⁶ And I will ask the Father, and he will give you another Advocate,[e] who will never leave you. ¹⁷ He is the Holy Spirit, who leads into all truth. The world cannot receive him, because it isn't looking for him and doesn't recognize him. But you know him, because he lives with you now and later will be in you.[f] ¹⁸ No, I will not abandon you as orphans—I will come to you. ¹⁹ Soon the world will no longer see me, but you will see me. Since I live, you also will live. ²⁰ When I am raised to life again, you will know that I am in my Father, and you are in me, and I am in you. ²¹ Those who accept my commandments and obey them are the ones who love me. And because they love me, my Father will love them. And I will love them and reveal myself to each of them."

Love Letters from God

The Anchor

You said you need to be grounded,
But yet you refuse the Anchor I left for you.

You said you feel alone and abandon,
But yet you refuse the Anchor I left for you.

You said you don't know which way to turn when you are troubled,
But yet you refuse the Anchor I left for you.

All you need to do is hold on to the Anchor I left for you.

All you have to do is turn to the Anchor I left for you.

Hold on tight to the Anchor I left for you,
And you will never move aimless again.

Psalmist Yvette Culver

Matthew 7:21-23

[21] "Not everyone who calls out to me, 'Lord! Lord!' will enter the Kingdom of Heaven. Only those who actually do the will of my Father in heaven will enter. [22] On judgment day many will say to me, 'Lord! Lord! We prophesied in your name and cast out demons in your name and performed many miracles in your name.' [23] But I will reply, 'I never knew you. Get away from me, you who break God's laws.'

Love Letters from God

Did You Say Yes?

Did you say yes,
Simply to please others.
Did you say yes,
Then hide and run for cover.

Did you say yes,
And mean it for the rest of your life.
Did you say yes,
Thinking there would be no strife.

Did you say yes,
Because it was expected of you.
Did you say yes,
Thinking you wouldn't have to go through.

When I said yes to you,
I never faltered or waivered.
Saying maybe or no to Me now,
Is simply unacceptable behavior.

So since you said yes,
You can no longer sit on the side.
So since you said yes,
My love for you will never die.

Psalmist Yvette Culver

Daniel 10:12

[12] *Then he continued, "Do not be afraid, Daniel. Since the first day that you set your mind to gain understanding and to humble yourself before your God, your words were heard, and I have come in response to them.*

Love Letters from God

Being HAD
(humbled and delivered)

Yes God, I want to be HAD

I kneel to the floor seeking Your face
To set myself free and dwell in Your space.

Yes God, I want to be HAD.

Psalmist Yvette Culver

Hosea 1:2-4

² When the LORD began to speak through Hosea, the LORD said to him, "Go, marry a promiscuous woman and have children with her, for like an adulterous wife this land is guilty of unfaithfulness to the LORD." ³ So he married Gomer daughter of Diblaim, and she conceived and bore him a son.

Gomer

Over 2000 years ago I was married to a man who loved me very much. Although, I didn't love him, at least not for a very long time. He was a prophet of Israel and God instructed him to find a harlot, a prostitute and to marry. I was the one he chose. Imagine how hard that might have been for him. To be a prophet and to be instructed to marry a woman no one would respect. How could people respect him with me as a wife? But my story is not that real story. God was using my life and my husband as a visual effect, a hands on effect for his people.

So we married and I gave birth to our son and God told my husband Hosea to name him Jezreel. Jezreel was both a city and territory in the heart of Israel. A place where much of the sin of Israel's history started. Jezreel means, God scatters, not worthy.

Our son was the reflection of Israel. Created by one parent who loved but born out of wickedness.

God named our second child Lo-Ruhamah.. Lo-ruhamah means to have no pity, no mercy. This child was a reflection of my life and the people of Israel. God was about to show us both that we had forsaken the ones who loved us and there would be a price to pay. Israel would be overtaken by the Assyrians, and I would be lost to my husband.

My third child was named Lo-ammi by God which means not mine. I say my third child because at this time I did not love Hosea and was not faithful. Hosea knew that this child was not his. So this child was God's way of showing Hosea that although he loved me, I did not return his love. Instead I chose to be with men who did not love me. Just as although God loved Israel, Israel chose to worship false gods.

I soon left Hosea for another man, and then another and then another. But these men did not love me as Hosea did and did not treat me the same way. Just as God did not desert Israel, Hosea did not desert me. Imagine, when me and my children were hungry, he made sure we were fed. And I wasn't living as his wife. He kept praying that my heart would change and would return to him. Just like God and Israel. But it did not and he finally had to cut me off. Just like God had to cut Israel off.

I was sold into slavery. Israel was overrun. I had betrayed my husband. Israel had betrayed God. I had been chosen by Hosea. Israel was God's chosen people.

But my God is a God of forgiveness. He instructed Hosea to get me out of slavery and to continue to pray for my heart to change. Eventually, my heart did change and because of that our children were changed. Lo-Ruhamah became Ruhamah ,which means Loved and Lo-Ammi became Ammi which means My People. Hosea forgave me, God forgave Israel. Hosea waited for my heart to change, God waited for the Israelites to change.
So you see, this isn't really about me. It's about how God can mold us to reflect an entire nation, to demonstrate through this earthly vessel the power of patience and forgiveness.

My name is Gomer, my name means completion and I am a vessel of clay formed by the Potter's hand.

Psalmist Yvette Culver

Psalms 62:5

¹I wait quietly before God,
   for my victory comes from him.
²He alone is my rock and my salvation,
   my fortress where I will never be shaken.
³So many enemies against one man—
   all of them trying to kill me.
To them I'm just a broken-down wall
   or a tottering fence.
⁴They plan to topple me from my high position.
   They delight in telling lies about me.
They praise me to my face
   but curse me in their hearts. Interlude
⁵Let all that I am wait quietly before God,
   for my hope is in him.
⁶He alone is my rock and my salvation,
   my fortress where I will not be shaken.
⁷My victory and honor come from God alone.
   He is my refuge, a rock where no enemy can reach me.
⁸O my people, trust in him at all times.
   Pour out your heart to him,
   for God is our refuge.

Silence

Don't be afraid of the silence,
Be still and let My voice be your guidance.

Let My words flood your veins,
Like the softness of a gentle rain.

Don't be afraid of what I have to say,
Know that I love you, but a healing needs to take place.

Stop trying to think ahead of Me,
You have no idea what I see.

This is a crucial time for you beloved,
For it is during the silence you can truly feel My love.

Galatians 5:22-25

²² But the fruit of the Spirit is love, joy, peace, forbearance, kindness, goodness, faithfulness, ²³ gentleness and self-control. Against such things there is no law. ²⁴ Those who belong to Christ Jesus have crucified the flesh with its passions and desires. ²⁵ Since we live by the Spirit, let us keep in step with the Spirit.

The Fruit of God's Labor

Don't get it twisted loved one,
I am the one who planted you in your mother's womb until you were done.
I planted you there for safety and security with plenty of **love**,
I gave you plenty of time to develop and grow as I watched you from above.

And don't worry my child, for I didn't forget where I planted you,
I was there at the moment it was time for you to push through.
Your life journey was just beginning and, you my creation gave me so much **joy,**
You were so pure and innocent, you were worth sacrificing my only Boy.

As you began to grow and experience the hardships of life,
I positioned myself to be your shield, to cover you when life rained with strife.
Whenever things seemed to come to you with ease,
That was Me holding you tightly to give you **peace**.
You've endured so much trying to stay on My path,
But I planted a good seed… with you, the devil don't stand a chance.
When I see you standing tall enduring the **longsuffering**,
I sprinkle a little more love on you, and act as your buffering.

You have accepted your purpose and I couldn't be more proud,
Look at you blossom, you have full command of the crowd
You speak My words with confidence, but a hint of **gentleness,**
For you know you can't reach someone who feels an offense.

As time went by I continued to prune you, to keep away the weeds,
If I saw you leaning over, not steady, not strong, I stood with you to provide your needs.
I surrounded you with those who you could run the race with, and not let you sit on the fence.
My garden is full of beautiful seeds who push each other towards **goodness**.
Now here you are, the Woman of God I created you to be,
Confident in who you serve…you know the devil is mad at Me.
Full of **meekness** and **temperance**, but more importantly **faith**,
You grow taller each day you wake and honestly seek My face.

So remember loved one, I planted you and I continue to nurture you,
I will sprinkle you with joy and water you with peace
I am the Spirit, you are the fruit of My labor.
And I have planted a good seed.

Psalmist Yvette Culver

2 Samuel 22:4

*"The LORD is my rock, my fortress, and my savior;
³ my God is my rock, in whom I find protection.
He is my shield, the power that saves me,
and my place of safety.
He is my refuge, my savior,
the one who saves me from violence.
⁴ I called on the LORD, who is worthy of praise,
and he saved me from my enemies.*

Love Letters from God

Hands Off!

You see that one right there,
The one praising My name everywhere, everyday, to everyone,
Keep your hands off My child!

You see that one on the hill,
The one that makes Me smile simply by following My will.
Keep your hands off My child!

You see the one shouting about My Glory so loud that her voice is gone,
Yes that one, the one you want to feel forlorn.
Keep your hands off my child!

I know you see her,
But you can't have her,
That is My child and she belongs to Me.

Pay close attention to My words,
Keep your hands off My child, for I have claimed her,
And she has claimed Me.

Psalmist Yvette Culver

Proverbs 3:11-12

*11 My child, don't reject the LORD's discipline,
and don't be upset when he corrects you.
12 For the LORD corrects those he loves,
just as a father corrects a child in whom he delights.*

Breaking

I will break you, but I will not forget you,
You vowed to follow Me and submit to My will,
so I'll wait until you do.

So I will break you until you cry out to Me,

For when you cry out to Me, you will begin to see,

That I have broken you, but, when I heal you,
you will be closer to Me.

Psalmist Yvette Culver

Psalms 150:1-6

[1] Praise the L{\sc ord}!
Praise God in his sanctuary;
praise him in his mighty heaven!
[2] Praise him for his mighty works;
praise his unequaled greatness!
[3] Praise him with a blast of the ram's horn;
praise him with the lyre and harp!
[4] Praise him with the tambourine and dancing;
praise him with strings and flutes!
[5] Praise him with a clash of cymbals;
praise him with loud clanging cymbals.
[6] Let everything that breathes sing praises to the L{\sc ord}!
Praise the L{\sc ord}!

Love Letters from God

Praise

Praise Women of God
Praise
Praise Him because you can't help it
Praise
Praise Him because you can't stop it
Praise
Praise Him because you can't control it
Praise
Praise Him til you feel His warmth envelope you
Praise
Praise Him til you reach that "other" realm
Praise
Praise Him til you speak your language only He understands
Praise Him
Praise Him
Him
Praise.

Genesis 21: 12-14

11 The matter distressed Abraham greatly because it concerned his son. 12 But God said to him, "Do not be so distressed about the boy and your slave woman. Listen to whatever Sarah tells you, because it is through Isaac that your offspring[b] will be reckoned. 13 I will make the son of the slave into a nation also, because he is your offspring."

Hagar – slave of Sarah

Son – Ishmael – her son with Abraham whose name means God hears.

I was a slave girl. I was a woman of no importance. My life was not my own and my needs were of no concern. Later in life I would discover just how wrong I was.

I was given to Sarah and Abraham to tend to their needs. Abraham was a wise and respected man and Sarah was a woman of great beauty. There came a point when Sarah and Abraham accepted the fact that she was too old to give Abraham an heir so she offered me to him in hopes that he would have a son.

Funny thing though, once I became with child, Sarah became distant and hateful. But this was her idea to begin with. But I know we all wish for things and then regret it when we actually get it.

The more my "condition" became obvious, the meaner Sarah became. One day I decided that I could not take anymore and made my escape heading back to my homeland of Egypt. And, I almost made it. I stopped by a spring of water at Shur. I was so tired. An angel appeared to me and told me that I needed to go back to Sarah, that my child would be a special child with a great future. A person of importance, unlike me. Believe me, it wasn't easy but I did go back.

Years went by and around the time my son was 14. Sarah became with child. At first, people doubted it was her child because of her age, but eventually they realized it was an act of God. Once Isaac was born to Sarah and Abraham, I was banished from the land I had called home for so many years. But I stuck to the promise of the Angel. That my child would have a great future.

We walked for days and soon the supplies that Abraham had given us ran out. I placed him under a tree and laid down a little further away and prepared for us to die. So I went before God for help and He answered.by showing me a well I had not noticed before. Only God. We eventually made our way to Paran where I raised my son who became the father of Arabia.

I am Hagar, mother of Ishmael, and I am a vessel of clay formed by the Potter's hand.

Deuteronomy 7:12

¹² *If you pay attention to these laws and are careful to follow them, then the LORD your God will keep his covenant of love with you, as he swore to your ancestors. ¹³ He will love you and bless you and increase your numbers. He will bless the fruit of your womb, the crops of your land—your grain, new wine and olive oil—the calves of your herds and the lambs of your flocks in the land he swore to your ancestors to give you.*

Love Letters from God

__Mirror Mirror__

If I asked you to stand before Me, in the same fashion that I created Adam and Eve, would you?
If I asked you to stand before Me with your arms wide, unashamed, knowing with Me, there's nowhere to hide, could you?

I need you to Peel back the fake layers, one painful strip at a time
I know it hurts My child, go ahead and cry

Now step in front of the mirror and see what I see,
Even those ugly scars are beautiful to Me

I need you to stare in the mirror, and don't you dare look away,
I've seen it all before, after all, I created you this way

You've been hiding long enough, it's time to face the truth
When others truly see you, do they love as I do?

When you truly see you, do you still love yourself,
Can you handle the scars you created yourself?

I love the side of you that you won't admit to, I love the you that makes you want to hide,
But with Me there's nowhere to run, so you might as well come inside.

Peel away the layers until you scream out in pain,
Only then can I begin to heal your shame.

When you finally stare in the mirror and see the true you,
Know that your reflection is Me, and I've always loved you.

Psalmist Yvette Culver

Esther 2:16-18

¹⁶ She was taken to King Xerxes in the royal residence in the tenth month, the month of Tebeth, in the seventh year of his reign. ¹⁷ Now the king was attracted to Esther more than to any of the other women, and she won his favor and approval more than any of the other virgins. So he set a royal crown on her head and made her queen instead of Vashti. ¹⁸ And the king gave a great banquet, Esther's banquet, for all his nobles and officials. He proclaimed a holiday throughout the provinces and distributed gifts with royal liberality.

Woman of God

Look at you, Woman of God
Just who do you think you are?
You walk with pride, glide with confidence
Commanding attention without even trying.
Wow, it's all over you
Joy, peace and love.
Who do you think you are?
It's quite obvious,
You are a Woman of God.

Did you see her over there?
Screaming and shouting like that.
What does she think people think when she does that?
How embarrassing.
Did you see her over there?
Praising God like she knows that she knows that she knows.
Embracing the fullness and love that He provides.
See her over there, that's a Woman of God.

Is that really her name?
WomanOfGod, WomanOfGod,
The joy you bring others just by being yourself,
The lives that you touch just by sharing your love of God
Being a servant of the Lord is not an easy task
It demands sacrifice, faith and dedication
But you do all that and much more I'm sure we don't know,
I heard someone call your name as if it were one word,
WomanOfGod, WomanOfGod, WomanOfGod.

Psalmist Yvette Culver

Jeremiah 29:11

[11] *For I know the plans I have for you," declares the* LORD, *"plans to prosper you and not to harm you, plans to give you hope and a future.* [12] *Then you will call on me and come and pray to me, and I will listen to you.* [13] *You will seek me and find me when you seek me with all your heart.*

Love Letters from God

Phenomenal

It's the touch of Your hand
It's the love that You show
It's that You comfort me to keep me from feeling low
I've been searching for answers, but You were there all the time
You my phenomenal God, will forever be mine.

It's the warmth that You give
It's the power You show… and believe me I know
It flows within me and allows me to grow
I cherish each day and sing Your praise
Because You are the phenomenal reason I live out each day.

For those who don't see, I hope soon that they will
That You are in charge and we're living out Your master plan
I feel You with every breath, with every heartbeat
I rise each day with the touch of Your hand
I praise Your power and know deep in my soul
That You are the phenomenal reason I live out this role.

Because You are who You are, and I am Your child
I no longer feel that my life is wild
I have come to realize, and praise be to thee
That I am phenomenal, because You made me.

Psalmist Yvette Culver

Romans 2:7

⁷ He will give eternal life to those who keep on doing good, seeking after the glory and honor and immortality that God offers.

Searching

Search for Me until you find Me,
Until you find Me you will not see My face.
You will not see My face unless you give yourself to Me.
Unless you give yourself to Me, I cannot heal you.
I cannot heal you until you ask Me for deliverance.
Until you ask Me for deliverance and walk in My answer I cannot restore you.
I cannot restore you unless you search for Me until you find Me
Until you find Me, I cannot give you peace.

I am here for you, I am here for you, I am waiting to give you peace.

Psalmist Yvette Culver

Matthew 1:19-21

19 Because Joseph her husband was faithful to the law, and yet[a] did not want to expose her to public disgrace, he had in mind to divorce her quietly. 20 But after he had considered this, an angel of the Lord appeared to him in a dream and said, "Joseph son of David, do not be afraid to take Mary home as your wife, because what is conceived in her is from the Holy Spirit. 21 She will give birth to a son, and you are to give him the name Jesus,[b] because he will save his people from their sins."

Mary

I grew up like any other girl in my land. I obeyed my parents, worked in the fields and gave reference and prayers to God. There was a young man from Bethlehem who had moved to my village and we were betrothed. I looked forward to being with him.

One day an angel told me that I would conceive a child through the Holy Spirit. Could it be true? Who would believe me? Would my future husband believe me? Why me? Why would God single me out of all the women He could use. But none of that mattered. It came to pass as the angel had spoken to me. My morals were questioned because I had not yet been with my husband. But after an angel visited him, he no longer questioned me. He stuck by me.

As the time grew near for my birth, we were summoned back to Bethlehem. You see, the king was afraid of the Messiah coming and had heard it would be a male child. He wanted to take count of the boys to find the Messiah. But my Father who had placed the seed would not let that happen.

I gave birth to my child and He was protected. God had used this simple girl. This girl of no consequence. This unworthy girl. I am the earthly mother of Jesus Christ.

I am Mary, from Nazareth, I am an earthen vessel filled with treasures.

Psalmist Yvette Culver

Matthew 27:55-57

⁵⁵ *Many women were there, watching from a distance. They had followed Jesus from Galilee to care for his needs.* ⁵⁶ *Among them were Mary Magdalene, Mary the mother of James and Joseph,[a] and the mother of Zebedee's sons.* ⁵⁷ *As evening approached, there came a rich man from Arimathea, named Joseph, who had himself become a disciple of Jesus.*

Silent Saturday

I didn't sleep last night. I kept replaying the whole thing in my head over and over. Like a bad dream. You see, I was there. I was there as they taunted Him as He tried to carry that cross up the hill. I was there when that man came out of the crowd and carried the cross up the hill for Him. I was there.

I can't really tell you how I ended up being there. I didn't even know Him, personally. The whole thing happened by accident. You see, I was getting water out of a well when I saw a crowd gathered. I was curious so I went to see what was going on. There was a Man there and He was the only one talking. The crowd around Him just listened. Listened in silence and everyone was only focused on Him. I pushed my way a little closer so I could hear Him. That's when it happened. I saw this Man, talking about the love of God and how we should treat each other. How we should love each other. I remember thinking. Who is this Man and why do I believe everything He's saying. There was something special about Him. I asked a man next to me who He was and he said, "He's the Teacher". Wow…I can't quite explain what happened next, but suddenly I wanted to hear everything He had to say. And more importantly, I believed everything He had to say. This Teacher, this Man, was pouring out more love than I had ever known.

Love Letters from God

From that point on I began to follow Him wherever He went. I was there when He destroyed the marketplace. I was there when they accused Him of blasphemy. I was there when they sentenced Him to die. I couldn't believe what was happening. I had finally found someone who made me believe in the one true God and now He was going to die.

I was there yesterday as they nailed Him to the cross and cried for Him with each blow. As they forced the crown of thorns in His head, as they pierced Him in the side, I cried. I didn't sleep last night and now I feel lost. What do I do now? Who do I follow now? The city feels, empty although there are plenty of people around. Something's missing. There is a silence around me that I can't explain. I can see people talking, but what they are saying sounds jumbled. I feel so empty! I can tell others feel it too. You can see who believed in Him just by looking at their face. They feel empty too. But I still believe what the Teacher said. Every word. I tried to stay close to the men who were close around Him but even they seem at a loss. The world is missing something. The World is dry.

I found out that some are going to His tomb to anoint His body. I plan to follow along. I know who this Teacher was. I know His connection to the true God and I just want to honor Him.

I pray I can sleep tonight.

Psalmist Yvette Culver

Joshua 2:1

2 Then Joshua son of Nun secretly sent two spies from Shittim. "Go, look over the land," he said, "especially Jericho." So they went and entered the house of a prostitute named Rahab and stayed there.

Rahab

I lived in Jericho at a time when the Israelites came to our city to swarm and destroy us. I was known by my people as being a harlot although my name means proud. There came a day when we all knew a battle was approaching. A battle in which we would fight against an army sent by God. This was God's army coming. The same army that He parted the Red Sea for when they fled Egypt. Being known as a harlot, a woman of disgrace, I have to admit I was a little surprised that I was the only one to understand and accept the power and love of God. I knew what would happen once they attacked us so when those two spies came to my house I hid them. The only thing I asked was that my family be spared of the oncoming slaughter. And as they came and attacked us, my family was the only family spared. Can you imagine? The harlot was spared. My God. The harlot was spared.

So I dwelt with the Israelites and soon married a man named Salmon. We had a son named Boaz who married Ruth from Moab. They had a son named Obed who had a son named Jesse who had a son name David, who became the King of Israel. Through twenty-six generations my descendent Jesus Christ was born.

I am Rahab, a harlot from Jericho, I am an earthen vessel filled with treasures.

Psalmist Yvette Culver

Ruth 2:8-12

⁸ So Boaz said to Ruth, *"My daughter, listen to me. Don't go and glean in another field and don't go away from here. Stay here with the women who work for me.* ⁹ *Watch the field where the men are harvesting, and follow along after the women. I have told the men not to lay a hand on you. And whenever you are thirsty, go and get a drink from the water jars the men have filled."* ¹⁰ *At this, she bowed down with her face to the ground. She asked him, "Why have I found such favor in your eyes that you notice me—a foreigner?"* ¹¹ *Boaz replied, "I've been told all about what you have done for your mother-in-law since the death of your husband—how you left your father and mother and your homeland and came to live with a people you did not know before.* ¹² *May the* LORD *repay you for what you have done. May you be richly rewarded by the* LORD, *the God of Israel, under whose wings you have come to take refuge."*

Ruth

I am originally from Moab where I met my husband who was from Bethlehem. He moved to Moab with his mother, father and brother. Our spiritual beliefs were different but we loved each other. It came to pass that my husband, his father and brother all died. My mother in law, Naomi decided to return to Bethlehem and although she insisted I stay with my people, when I married my husband, his people became my people, so her people were also now my people. I vowed to stay with her wherever she would go.

So we went to her homeland, penniless and depending on the kindness of family. I worked in the fields gleaning from the thrashing floor. A much older kinsman of Naomi let it be known that I should not be harmed, for it was known that although the wheat on the ground was not recovered, the workers would often run off those following behind them to collect it for food.

I eventually let it be known to this older man, Boaz, that I should become his wife. He accepted. We became the parents of many children and one son we named Obed. Obed had a son named Jesse who had a son named David who became the King of Israel, whose descendants became the earthly parents of my descendant Jesus Christ.

I am Ruth, from Moab, I am an earthen vessel filled with treasures.

Psalmist Yvette Culver

Exodus 15:3

"The LORD is my strength and my defense[a];
he has become my salvation.
He is my God, and I will praise him,
my father's God, and I will exalt him.
³ The LORD is a warrior;
the LORD is his name.

<u>Woman, Warrior, Worshipper</u>

Divide the room into three groups of women.

I am a woman, created by God.
But don't misunderstand, I was not created as an afterthought.
I was created to finish the work God began when He created Adam.
So, I was not an afterthought.
I am the vessel designated by God to carry and birth mankind.
Think about it. God created Adam and Eve, so He could have created the rest of mankind.
But He trusted me. He trusted me to carry His son.
He trusted me, woman.
I am a woman created by God, and I am not an afterthought.

I am a – group 1 response "Woman"

I am a warrior, created by God.
We go into spiritual battle for ourselves and others.
When God created us He created a woman warrior who is not afraid to go to battle.
We go into battle every day that we praise and worship God.
I am a woman warrior created by God, and I am not an afterthought.

I am a - group 1 response "Woman" – then group 2 response "Warrior"

I am a worshipper, created by God
I was created to praise Him and that is my purpose.
We were the ones to stay with Him until the very end and worship Him.
We were the ones to go to the tomb to worship Him and discovered He was not there.
We were the ones to birth Him. How could we not naturally worship Him.
I am a woman warrior worshipper created by God, and I am not an afterthought.

I am a – group 1 response "Woman" – then group 2 response "Warrior" – then group 3 response "Warrior".

Point to each group for their response and build to a chant of " Woman Warrior Worshipper".

After about 5 times end with

And I am not an afterthought!

YOUR LOVE LETTERS TO GOD

Love Letters from God

Psalmist Yvette Culver

Love Letters from God

Psalmist Yvette Culver

Love Letters from God

Psalmist Yvette Culver

Love Letters from God

Psalmist Yvette Culver

Psalmist Yvette Culver

Stay Blessed!

Psalmist Yvette Culver

ABOUT THE AUTHOR

Yvette Culver is a native of Los Angeles, California and currently lives in Dallas, Texas. She has worked in the Entertainment Industry for over 20 years. In 2012, Ms. Culver published her first book, *God Drops*, and in the same year founded Theatrical Learning Center, a non-profit youth Entertainment Training Program and iamHisfoundation, a service organization. In 2014 iamHisfoundation launched its first program, The Breakfast Club, whose mission is to serve those who serve others.

Psalmist Yvette Culver is an inspirational speaker and strives to be HAD (humbled and delivered) by God.